When the world was full of all these amazing and lovely things, God made people.

"Take care of my world," God told them. "It is a good world and it will give you all you need."

Noah and the flood

What a mess people made of the world!

God spoke to Noah. "You're the only good man left," said God. "Your job is to save the world for a new beginning.

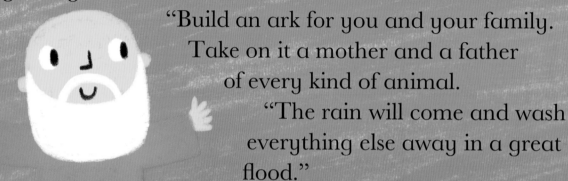

"Build an ark for you and your family. Take on it a mother and a father of every kind of animal.

"The rain will come and wash everything else away in a great flood."

When the flood came, everyone on the ark was safe.
At last the flood went down.
"Look at the rainbow," said God. "It's time to start the world again. I promise to keep it safe."

Baby Moses

Down by the riverside, Miriam watched.

Would anyone see the basket she and her mother had hidden? Her baby brother was sleeping inside it. Would the wicked king's soldiers find him and harm him?

They did not. The princess found the basket and the baby.
"I love him!" she said. "I am going to name him Moses.
Now, who could look after him for me?"

Miriam stepped
forward. "I can find
someone!" she said.

She brought her mother.
Moses grew up safe and good.

Brave David

Goliath was the champion of the enemy army.
His weapons were the best, the sharpest,
the scariest.

"Ha ha ha!" he laughed. "If you can beat me,
your side wins the war.

"But you're all too scared. Ha ha ha!"

"I'm not scared," said David. "I may only be a shepherd boy with a stick and sling, but I trust in God."
He slung a stone.
Goliath fell down. David had won!

Jonah in deep trouble

Why was Jonah in the sea? Because the sailors had thrown him off the boat.

Why did they do that? Because God had sent a storm to stop Jonah sailing far away.

God sent a big fish to swallow Jonah up.

Deep inside the fish, Jonah understood. "I'm sorry I disobeyed you, God," he said.

The fish threw Jonah onto the shore. Jonah did what he knew God wanted: he went to Nineveh.

"Listen, all you wicked people," he cried. "Say sorry to God. Change your ways. Or else!"

The people said sorry. God forgave them.

God always forgives those who say sorry.

Daniel and the lions

Daniel was a good man. Every day, he did a good job for the king. Every day, he said prayers to God.

Wicked men got him into trouble. The law said he must be thrown to the lions.

God did not forget Daniel. God sent an angel to lull the lions to sleep all through the night.

In the morning, the king came to see. "Daniel's safe!" he cried. "His God has taken care of him."

Baby Jesus

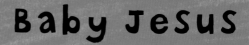

On the hills near Bethlehem, shepherds
were guarding their sheep.
   An angel appeared.
   "Good news," said the angel. "Everything changes
from tonight. There is a baby born in Bethlehem who
is God's chosen king.
   "Go and see."

The shepherds went. In a stable, with the animals, they found Mary and Joseph and little baby Jesus.

"Astonishing news," said the wise men. "There is a new star. It is a sign that a great king has been born."

It led them to Bethlehem. The wise men gave gold and frankincense and myrrh: royal gifts for God's newborn king.

The two builders

Jesus grew up. He told people how to live as God's friends: loving and forgiving.

"If you obey my teaching, you are like the wise builder. He chose a place high on a rock for his house.

"The storm came. The wind blew. The flood rose.

"The wise man's house was safe.

"If you don't obey my teaching, you are like the foolish builder. He chose a place on the sand by the river.

"The storm came. The wind blew. The flood rose.

"The foolish man's house fell down.

"What a crash!"

Jesus and the children

All kinds of people came to see Jesus. Some wanted to listen. Some wanted to ask questions.

Some of the people were grown up and important.

So when some mothers came with their children, Jesus' friends said, "Stop! Jesus is busy with important people."

Jesus heard them.

"Let the children come to me," he said. "Don't try to stop them.

"The kingdom of heaven belongs to such as these."

The lost sheep

Sometimes people get their whole life in a muddle.
Does God love them and forgive them? Jesus told a story.
  "A shepherd had 100 sheep. One went missing.
  "He left the 99 safely grazing and went looking.

"When he found his lost sheep, he was as happy as could be. He carried it home and put it with the flock.

"He called his friends. 'Come and have a party. I found my lost sheep.'

"God is like that shepherd," said Jesus. "When someone who has lost their way comes back to God, all the angels sing."

The way to heaven

Not everyone liked Jesus. They didn't believe he was God's king. They didn't like forgiving very much either.

They told lies about Jesus. They had him put to death on a cross.

Jesus' friends thought it was the end of everything. Love… forgiveness… heaven.